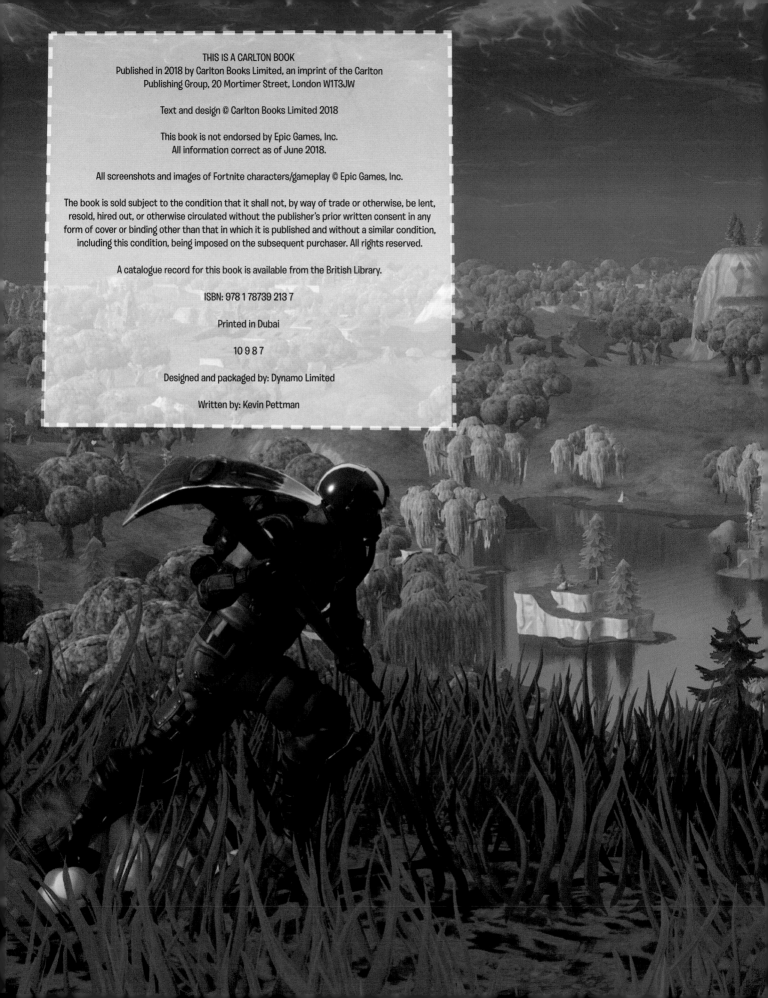

THIS IS A CARLTON BOOK

Published in 2018 by Carlton Books Limited, an imprint of the Carlton
Publishing Group, 20 Mortimer Street, London W1T3JW

Text and design © Carlton Books Limited 2018

This book is not endorsed by Epic Games, Inc.
All information correct as of June 2018.

All screenshots and images of Fortnite characters/gameplay © Epic Games, Inc.

A catalogue record for this book is available from the British Library.

ISBN: 978 1 78739 213 7

Printed in Dubai

10 9 8 7

Designed and packaged by: Dynamo Limited

Written by: Kevin Pettman

FORTNITE

BATTLE ROYALE

ULTIMATE WINNER'S GUIDE

CARLTON
BOOKS

CONTENTS

Good move - you've locked onto your ultimate survivor's guide to the biggest and best battle game in the Universe! Fortnite is full of action, adventure, skill, tactics, survival, building, takedowns and much, much more.

Whether you're a total beginner or a Fortnite pro, this epic book will turn you into an awesome gamer. It's packed with secrets, tips, guides, facts and fun. Prepare for battle, guys!

06 >>>> **14 Things You Need to Know!**

08 >>>> **Hero Time!**

10 >>>> **Take Control**

12 >>>> **On the Map**

14 >>>> **In the Firing Line**

16 >>>> **Basic Battle Tips**

18 >>>> **Beginner Dos and Don'ts**

20 >>>> **Say What?!**

22 >>>> **Safety First**

24 >>>> **Boss Battle Royale**

26 >>>> **Land Like a Pro**

28 >>>> **The Storm!**

30 >>>> **Be a Brilliant Builder**

32 >>>> **Become a Weapons Master!**

33 >>>> **Close Range**

34 >>>> **Medium Range**

35 >>>> **Long Range**

36 >>>> **Looking For Loot**

38 >>>> **Advanced Battle Tips**

40 >>>> **Close-up Combats**

42 >>>> **Trap Tricks and Tips**

44 >>>> **Specials and Secrets**

46 >>>> **Team Up!**

48 >>>> **In-game Extras**

Spot the Ultra Rare Golden Llama

Fortnite players **dream** of being in the right place when a **loot llama** appears. And few have seen a golden one, but can you find it **hidden** in the pages of this book?

By the way – the one in plain sight on page 61 **doesn't** count!

50 >>>> **Planet Attack!**

52 >>>> **Know the Enemy**

54 >>>> **Rescue Survivors**

56 >>>> **Crafting and Building**

58 >>>> **Weapons at the Ready!**

60 >>>> **Save the World**

62 >>>> **My Fortnite Records, Faves and Facts**

64 >>>> **Epic Emotes!**

STAYING SAFE ONLINE:

Fortnite is an online game where users play against gamers of different ages from **around the world**. Gamers can interact and communicate using the in-game chat and text feature. The voice chat can be **turned off**. Parents should talk to their child about staying safe online and ask their child to tell them if something has upset them. Player behaviour can be **reported** to the Fortnite game makers. **See pages 22 and 23 for more safety advice.**

14 things you need to know about

FORTNITE

Get the lowdown on the game that everyone is playing with these essential facts...

1 **Save the World** and **Battle Royale** are two different versions of the game. Battle Royale was the first to be free to play.

2 Battle Royale is a **100-player** contest. The last hero standing takes the **Victory Royale crown!**

3 Fortnite can be played across **Xbox, PlayStation, Nintendo Switch, PC, Mac** and some mobiles and tablets.

4 Characters can do cool **dance emotes** - including **The Floss!**

5 In **Save The World**, players form a team with up to three others. You complete missions and square up to scary zombie monsters, known as **husks!**

6 In the UK, Fortnite has a **12 certificate.**

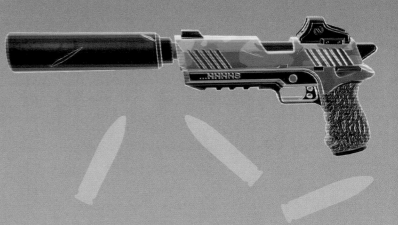

7 Weapons are found in chests, supply drops and on the ground. An **orange glowing weapon** is very rare - snatch it and Victory Royale could be yours!

8 It's not all about looting and shooting. In Fortnite, **building** structures can help you pick off enemies, protect yourself and stay in the game longer.

9 Players must stay inside the **storm eye**, which shrinks as the game develops. Get caught outside it and you'll take serious damage!

10 **Looting** lets you collect cool weapons and items. Search through houses and structures for secret stashes of game-changing items.

11 The in-game currency in Fortnite is called **V-Bucks**.

12 Most gamers wear **headsets** to hear things like other footsteps, supply drops and the twinkling of chests!

13 Fortnite is made by Epic Games and over **40 million** gamers have already downloaded Battle Royale. Wow!

14 As well as playing solo against 99 others, players can also team up in **duos** or **squads** with three others.

HERO TIME!

These first few pages are all about the basics. It's time to learn about the heroes you play and the cool character skins to dress them in!

FORTNITE FACT!

View all the skins you have by clicking the Locker tab.

Random Royale

In Fortnite Battle Royale, the hero you control is **randomly** given to you. But don't stress because all the heroes have **the same powers and abilities**! If you play as a mega-muscled fighter or a sleek and skilful female, it's your **weapons and tactics** that will ultimately get you through the battle.

Super Skins

You can make your hero look different (and much cooler!) by upgrading their **skin**, which means your character's outfit. Do this by using your V-Bucks to buy skins through the Item Shop tab. But remember, skins still don't improve your game play and are just **cosmetic**. Here are five of Fortnite's best...

Red Knight

Rarity: Legendary

Part of the Fort Knights set, stick this outfit on to declare yourself the **red menace** of Anarchy Acres!

Wukong

Rarity: Legendary

Also known as the **Monkey King**, this skin was introduced to celebrate Chinese New Year.

Arctic Assassin

Rarity: Rare

From the **ice-cool** Arctic Command set, you'll stay frosty inside this sick grey battle getup!

Burnout

Rarity: Epic

This scary black and red leather combo is bound to **put fear** into your opponents.

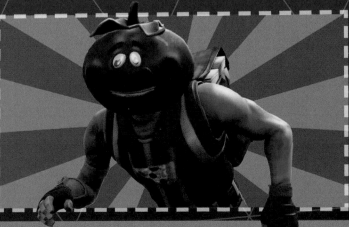

Tomatohead

Rarity: Epic

Fans of Tomato Temple love this skin that looks just like the **pizza restaurant's mascot!**

 FORTNITE FACT!

Unleash dance moves, like **The Dab** or **The Chicken**, by selecting them in the Item Shop.

TAKE CONTROL

If you're new to the action, you'll need to get to grips with the standard Battle Royale controls...

FIRST LOOK

Click on **Settings** in the top right of your screen, then scroll to the **Wireless Controller tab**. You'll be shown the layout controls for playing Battle Royale on your platform. **Study these carefully**, especially basic functions like moving, sprinting, weapon aiming, weapon selecting and jumping.

QUIET TIME

To get up to speed with **controlling your hero**, try landing in a very quiet and remote spot on the island **next to the ocean**. If there are no enemies around and you can loot a weapon, start using the controls to shoot and build. Don't worry if the storm wipes you out as this is just **valuable practice time** as you learn the basics!

LOBBY PRACTICE

Before the battle bus takes off, you'll get a small amount of time to roam in the lobby area. Use this time to practise the controls, try some basic building functions, or just try jumping and crouching. It's a **good warm up** before you land on the island.

BUILDER PRO

Using the Builder Pro **console setting** means you can build much more quickly in the game. You can construct a life-saving ramp or wall in the **blink of an eye** without having to tap a stack of buttons!

VICTORY DANCE

Dancing isn't a **vital** part of gameplay, but it's awesome to show off some slick bounces and have a laugh! On Xbox and PS4, the down arrow on D-Pad busts out your dance emotes. Have a practice in the lobby area.

Discover the basic bits of your gaming screen...

 The left box shows ammo loaded into your weapon, with ammo you have remaining on the right.

 24 | 34

 Health (green) and shield (blue) points.

50   100
100   100

 Your compass.

SW   **W**   NW
240 250   285 300

 Number of players remaining in the battle (left) and kills you've made (right).

 72   0

 Your inventory items, including weapons and shield potions.

ON THE MAP

Get to know the sickest locations
on the Battle Royale map!

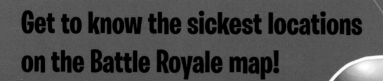

JUNK JUNCTION

HAUNTED HILLS

RISKY REELS

LAZY LINKS

WAILING WOODS

TOMATO TEMPLE

LOOT LAKE

LONELY LODGE

SNOBBY SHORES

TILTED TOWERS

DUSTY DIVOT

RETAIL ROW

GREASY GROVE

SALTY SPRINGS

SHIFTY SHAFTS

PARADISE PALMS

FATAL FIELDS

FORTNITE FACT!

The map can **change**
from season to season...
who knows what you'll
find next!

FLUSH FACTORY

LUCKY LANDING

Wailing Woods

Navigate through the **vast trees** to find the secret centre bunker, and make sure you collect as much wood as you can - **you will need it later!**

Tilted Towers

Battle Royale's **biggest town** is stuffed with useful materials and loot. It's always stuffed with other gamers too, so **stay super alert!**

Greasy Grove

It **can become crowded**, so use the house and buildings as cover to check the scene before you loot and shoot in Greasy Grove!

Paradise Palms

Head to the racecourse in this **desert paradise** and try out the All Terrain Kart (ATK) which came in the season five update.

Haunted Hills

Don't get **spooked** out at the cemetery in Haunted Hills! Sometimes it can be **dead quiet** here.

Salty Springs

One of the most **popular** drop zones on the map! Keep an eye out for houses to loot and a **mysterious treasure map**.

Tomato Temple

This wacky temple is full of **helpful loot**. Grabbing a range of weapons early on is a great tactic, as long as you can can find your way around!

Retail Row

Shops, houses, buildings - this is a **great location** to quickly load up with loot at the beginning of a battle!

Lucky Landing

Drop into the south and **swipe all you can** from Lucky Landing. It's not huge but there's helpful loot to discover.

IN THE FIRING LINE

When you're racing to gather arms, it's good to know what to look out for, and what to drop!

Assault Rifle

Rarity: Rare

FAN FAVOURITE!

DPS*: 181.5
*Damage Per Second

Damage: 33

Reload time: 2.2

Magazine size: 30

Lots of players say the assault rifle is the **best all-round gun**. It's good in close and medium-range battles, with sharp accuracy and decent damage. The rare assault rifle is **not too difficult to find** and is definitely a weapon to keep hold of!

Players begin with a health of 100HP, plus a shield bar that can add an extra 100HP.

Take damage and your health suffers.

Shield potion
+50 shield

Slurp juice
Heals 25HP
+25 shield

Bandages
Heals 15HP

Pistol

The common pistol is okay at close range, but even then it is outgunned by shotguns. It's a weapon you'll **dump as soon as poss!**

Rarity: Common

DPS: 155.25

Damage: 23

Reload time: 1.5

Magazine size: 16

Pump Shotgun

If you're suddenly **face to face with an opponent**, a blast on this shotgun will soon show who's the boss!

Rarity: Uncommon

DPS: 66.5

Damage: 95

Reload time: 4.6

Magazine size: 5

Tactical Shotgun

This weapon looks pretty good in combat and if you get your aim right, it'll cause **pretty good damage** too!

Rarity: Rare

DPS: 111

Damage: 74

Reload time: 5.7

Magazine size: 8

Bolt-action Sniper Rifle

Awesome damage, but you **need a great aim** because this weapon must be reloaded after each bullet!

Rarity: Rare

DPS: 34.7

Damage: 105

Reload time: 3.0

Magazine size: 1

Thermal Scoped Assault Rifle

Found in both epic and legendary, use its **thermal heat-seeking powers** to see chests, supply drops and enemy heat signals!

Rarity: Legendary

DPS: 66.6

Damage: 37

Reload time: 2.07

Magazine size: 15

BASIC BATTLE TIPS

Take the high ground

Get above a location to see what, and who, is around. It's also **harder for others to hit you** up there!

Ramp it up

Building ramps to reach roofs or to take you high over the ground is a **great survival tip**.

Set a trap

Loot a trap item, then set it inside a building for an unsuspecting player following you to set off. **Boom!**

Take a peek

Look carefully around corners before you enter a room. It's a **simple tip** but taking a peek can be a life saver!

Crouch down

Crouching makes you a **smaller target** to hit and helps steady your weapon aim. You're quieter in this pose as well.

FORTNITE FACT!

If you spot a **red apple** on the ground near an apple tree, consume it and you'll get a **plus five** health boost!

Loot long-range weapons

Pick up sniper and automatic rifles **as soon as you can**. These weapons will be needed for long-range strikes.

Don't fire too early

Only shoot when you're sure you can take the other player out. Remember that **blasting bullets** also alerts others that you're there!

Stay in the storm

Think of the storm circle on the map as the **safe zone**. Stay inside it to keep your health up.

BEGINNER DOS...

Here are five vital tips to mastering Battle Royale. It's time to be the king or queen of the Fortnite map!

DO USE SHIELD POTIONS!

Always drink **one as soon as you find it** to increase your shield by 50.

DO HAVE ENOUGH TIME!

Before battle, make sure you have **enough time** to play. The game won't wait while you have dinner!

DO GET INTO 1v1s!

Practise **tense** player-v-player battles - you'll need to master them if you want to be a pro.

DO BE PATIENT!

It takes a lot of practice and learning to boss Battle Royale. **Build your skills slowly** and it'll be worth it in the end!

DO COLLECT RESOURCES!

When you're not looting or shooting, **bash away** at things like trees, cars and containers to harvest as many building resources as possible.

BEGINNER DON'TS...

Whatever your gameplay style, make sure you remember these key Fortnite no-nos!

DON'T FORGET AMMO BOXES!

It's awesome to collect epic new weapons, but remember that you need **plenty** of ammunition too!

DON'T WORRY ABOUT KILLS!

The aim of Battle Royale is to be the last person standing, **not** how many people you take out. Never forget that!

DON'T ELIMINATE YOURSELF!

If you do a dumb thing like explode a rocket launcher right in front of yourself, you're **outta the game**, pal!

DON'T RUSH TO LOOT!

It's tempting to loot straight after you eliminate a player, but **check it's safe** to venture out as others may be lurking!

DON'T STAY IN THE OPEN!

Hanging out in open fields is a **bad move**. Always try to stay low, hidden, quiet and on the move from potential snipers.

SAY WHAT?!

Get to know the essential Fortnite phrases and words...

BATTLE BUS

The flying blue bus that **all gamers** jump from at the beginning of Battle Royale.

PvP

Player versus Player. Battle Royale is a PvP game. Save the World is Player versus **Environment** (PvE).

SUPPLY DROP

A blue loot crate that falls randomly inside the storm. It has **better items** than a regular chest.

HARVESTING

When a player **collects resources** like wood, metal and brick. Crucial if you want to be a master builder!

SPAWN

Spawning means when things like **weapons, resources and items** are created on the map.

LTM

Limited Time Mode. These are **special games** only available for a limited time, like 50 vs 50 and Solo Showdown.

VICTORY ROYALE

Awarded to the eventual winner of the game. Victory Royale is your **ultimate aim!**

TAKEDOWN

When you take an opponent out of the game. Also known as a **kill**.

CHUG JUG

A **legendary** Fortnite item! Consume this to restore your health and shield.

SNIPER

Someone who fires at you from a **long distance**. Snipers need to have a very accurate shot.

CHEST

In Battle Royale, wooden chests contain items like **weapons and potions** which can be looted.

SKINS

The appearance of your hero (game character). **Customizing skins** is a big part of Fortnite.

MED KIT

A very handy healing item that restores **all health** in ten seconds.

UPDATES

When game makers Epic change or add something **new** to Fortnite. Updates are usually pretty sick!

GLIDER

Players **deploy** their glider after jumping from the Battle Bus and use it to drop down to a location.

LOOT LLAMA

An extremely rare (and **extremely weird** looking!) loot supply full of materials, traps, potions, ammo and more.

SAFETY FIRST

Fortnite is a fun and adventurous game, but it's very important to stay safe while playing online.

PARENT PLAY

If you're old enough to play Fortnite, it's a good idea to **show your parents or guardians** what the game is about. Let them watch you play - better still, take it in turns to have a game and battle together!

FORTNITE FACT!

Language filters can be applied in **Settings**. Voice chat can be turned off in the **Audio tab**.

SOUND IT OUT

You may use headphones when you play, but having the sound turned up on your **TV or monitor** means other people in your house can hear what's going on and being said. That can reassure them that nothing inappropriate is being said.

PASSWORD POWER

When setting up an account, it's a good idea to use a **new and strong password**. Never share passwords with anyone online.

USERNAME INFO

In online games like Fortnite, never create a username that could give away any of your personal details to other people. **Don't use your first name and surname together.**

TRACK TIME

With your parents, it's good advice to set an **agreed time limit** on how long you should play Fortnite for. This means you'll know exactly how long you have to enter a battle. Taking a **screen break** can stop you becoming too tired.

SMART CHAT

Fortnite lets you chat and type messages to other players. **Never give away information about yourself to others**, especially if you don't know them in real life. Always tell an adult if you are unhappy or unsure about things you hear or see.

REPORT IT

In the main menu, potential bad player behaviour can be **reported** to Epic. Sending screengrabs or video of bad behaviour helps Epic see what has happened.

GAME GUIDE

'Etiquette' is the fancy word describing how players should behave to others. Interact with gamers politely and **don't use bad language**. If you cheat, you're likely to be reported and possibly **banned** by the game makers. Not good.

BOSS BATTLE ROYALE

Now that you've seen the basics and discovered some top tips, it's time to crank it up! This part of your Fortnite guide reveals all the special secrets and techniques you need to boss a battle. Accept the mission and crack on!

LAND LIKE A PRO

Deadly Drop Zone Details!

Work out what your options are once you've boarded the battle bus.

Getting to the ground quickly means you can begin looting ASAP! Aim for a **low spot**, like a road or valley, and stay away from hills - high spots will make your glider open sooner. Dive-bombing is **much quicker** than gliding.

! **FORTNITE FACT!**

Don't land in the water around the island - you'll instantly **eliminate** yourself!

Before jumping from the bus, know the location you want to hit. Don't jump out **directly over the top** of your chosen location. Gliding down in a straight line is **slow** compared to moving at an angle!

Once you're close to the ground, aim for a raised structure or a rooftop. You'll have a **view** over your immediate area and can **loot** the building for your all-important first weapon and shield potion.

Wherever the bus starts from on the map usually sees more players land there. You can stay onboard longer and **choose a quieter spot** away from other gamers and hopefully **score some rare loot!**

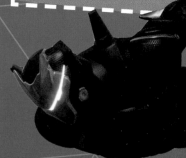

As you're gliding in, keep a **watchful eye** on other players who are dropping at the same time. Try to see where they land and how many there are – these are your **rivals** for Victory Royale!

Land like a legend...

 ! Know where you're aiming for.

 ! Get to ground super speedily.

 ! Loot a weapon straight away.

7 Secrets to Surviving

THE STORM!

FORTNITE FACT!

Remember that in every match, the storm eye will move in a **random direction**. Master all the potential stormy movements.

1. Pay attention to the **automatic alerts** that appear, telling you when the storm eye will **shrink**. You'll know how quickly you need to move to keep inside it!

2. You could stay **close to the edge** of the storm, then move slowly in with it as it shrinks. You can pick up kills and hope to reach the **last ten** this way.

3. **Don't get stuck** inside a building having a gunfight if you need to rush out to reach the safe zone. **Plan your tactics in advance** and know your **escape routes**!

4. On your map, the **blue circle** shows the current eye of the storm, and the **white circle** shows you where the eye of the storm will be next. **Keep checking both.**

5. If your first battle action and looting is a long way from the storm eye, you're gonna do **a lot of running** to make it inside. Never be too far away from the white circle!

6. A shield potion does not defend you against **storm damage**, which hits health directly. Uh oh!

7. Know what damage the storm will do. In the final stages it will cause 10DPS and zap your health in **no time**!

Be a Brilliant
BUILDER

To go deep into Battle Royale, you need to learn how, and what, to build!

There are three building materials to harvest in Battle Royale - **wood, brick** and **metal**. The level you have of each is shown on the right of your screen. Wood is the **best all-round building resource**, and you can build quickly with it, but the other two are stronger.

Wood

Brick

Metal

To harvest materials, or 'mats', simply **smash something** such as a wall or car with your pickaxe and watch your inventory boost. If you make a kill, you can also loot the person you defeated and **take their building mats.**

FORTNITE FACT!

When striking with your pickaxe, keep hitting the **flashing circle** that appears and you'll gather that material quicker.

Shield Walls

As you run through open spaces where **others can easily shoot you**, quickly building wooden shield walls as you move can keep you safe. Place the protective walls to the front, rear or side of you.

Fort Fight

Building a tall fort is a **top technique** to get height and fighting advantage over the oppo! Don't make it too big or detailed as you'll move on when the storm eye shrinks. **Add windows** so you can easily shoot at other players.

Port-a-fort Power

The epic rarity port-a-fort item is a **glowing cube** that, when deployed, instantly builds a **big metal fort**. It's both super cool and super helpful in the final stages!

FORTNITE FACT!

Top players will aim to have **over 300** of each building material, especially in the later stages of a battle.

Fence Fight

Small wooden fences may not look great, but they're **mega quick** to build and can give you a vital shield. Low fences aren't easy to see so they don't give away your location. They can make an **ace shooting spot**.

Raise the Roof

As battle draws to a close and opponents pick up grenades and rockets, your building or fort should have a **roof**. This will help reduce damage from missiles blasted at you.

Become a Weapons
MASTER

These pages reveal how to get the best from your guns. Whether your opponent's right in your face or far away, you'll soon be eliminating them like a pro!

Weapon Essentials...

 Always be alert to who's around when you get into a gun fight

 Epic and the even rarer legendary weapons can be very similar

 Using short bursts of fire can improve your accuracy

Close Range

Best weapon: Heavy Shotgun

Dropped into Battle Royale in 2018, gamers instantly went nuts for this awesome weapon! The legendary heavy shotgun is obviously not as easy to find as the pump or tactical, but it's well worth searching for and looting.

★ ★ ★ ★ ★

Rarity: Legendary and epic

DPS: 77

Damage: 77

Fire rate: 1.0

Reload time: 5.6

Magazine size: 7

In **close-range** shootouts it's the **best all round**. The pump delivers a little more damage but the heavy, in legendary and epic class, whips out greater DPS and two more bullets in the clip.

Look for the heavy in chest and supply drops and you may be able to loot it after a takedown. **Take a split second longer to aim up** a shot because this blaster needs an accurate bullet to inflict **breathtaking damage**.

! FORTNITE FACT!

The heavy shotgun was the **first legendary shotgun** in Battle Royale.

Also use: pump shotgun, tactical shotgun, suppressed submachine gun

Medium Range

Best weapon: Assault Rifle SCAR

Even though it's pretty special from distance too, the assault rifle SCAR is the absolute boss of mid-range duels! If you clap eyes on this somewhere on the map, do all you can to loot it and place in your inventory. The SCAR is a beefed up model of the M16.

★★★★★

Rarity: Legendary and epic

DPS: 198

Damage: 36

Fire rate: 5.5

Reload time: 2.1

Magazine size: 30

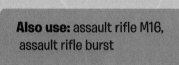

Also use: assault rifle M16, assault rifle burst

You don't need to be a crack shot to **get to grips with this monster,** but a headshot can almost wipe out an opponent in one hit. Its large mag size keeps you firing for a long time, but even then the reload time is not that long.

Be aware that there's really not much difference between a purple epic SCAR rifle and the sparkly orange legendary. If you have the purple flavour, be happy that **this rifle can fire you into a top ten shootout!**

Long Range

Best weapon: Semi-auto Sniper Rifle

The bolt-action sniper rifle (page 15) has slightly better stats, but for picking targets at distance, the semi-auto is most gamers' preferred weapon. Its clip is ten times bigger than the bolt-action, which means less reloading, and reload time is also a little sharper.

Rarity:	Uncommon and rare
DPS:	90
Damage:	75
Fire rate:	1.2
Reload time:	2.3
Magazine size:	10

! **FORTNITE FACT!**

Sniper rifles need heavy ammo, which you'll **need to keep topped up** as you loot.

Impressive damage will be unleashed from the rifle if you **treat the trigger lightly** – don't fire off too many bullets at once. It has **a lot of recoil** and you'll need a fraction of a second to steady your aim.

You'll need to **stay zoomed in** to lock in on your opponent. But because it can fire off multiple shots, you'll be standing still for a bit longer than with other weapons and you could make yourself an **easy target**!

Also use: hunting rifle, bolt-action sniper rifle

LOOKING FOR LOOT

There are certain places you should head for or keep an eye out for in your search for the best gear to help you battle like a pro!

Check the Roofs...

The beginning of a battle is the **best time** to enter buildings and houses. You have a good chance of being the **first to find** chests and loot much-needed weapons. Make sure you go all the way to the roof as you loot - you may need to build ramps and bust walls to reach these spots.

...and Basements!

Don't forget to go down as well as up! You can **harvest a stack of helpful items** in a basement, and many gamers forget to go there. Look for basement entrances to **smash through**, which saves you having to enter through the main part of a house.

Supply from the Sky

Supply drops are **blue crates** that land from the sky by balloon. They can often spawn when the game's down to 20 to 30 players. When you **hear a noise like thunder**, look up to see where the drop will come down and make your way over for the goodies!

Awesome Ammo

Ammo chests are **very important**. These dark green boxes can be tough to spot when you're rushing through a location, but always **take a second** to top up your ammo stash!

VIP Vehicles

Think cars and trucks aren't worth a second look? **Think again**! Keep an eye out for chests around, or on the top of, cars. Loot can also be **hidden in the back of trucks** - just make sure you're not trapped inside and taken out in a gunfight.

Look Again

Loot is not always hidden in the same places! It's worth looking in **secret spots** where you've seen chests and ammo boxes before, but don't expect it to always be there. In Battle Royale, you need a backup plan and **sharp eyes** to discover the best items!

 FORTNITE FACT!

You can use a **launch pad trap** to get in the air and deploy your glider to drop onto the supply drop balloon. **Mega cool** way to loot!

3 ace loot locations: ⟨⟨⟨⟨⟨⟨

 **Tilted Towers**    **Retail Row**    **Tomato Temple**

ADVANCED BATTLE TIPS

Tracer trail

Bullets fired in Fortnite leave a tracer trail, so you can **see the direction they've been shot from**. This helps you identify where long-range attackers are. But remember the trace also gives away your location when you've shot your weapon!

Close doors

Sometimes it's a smart move to close doors behind you after you enter a building. Leaving doors open could **alert other gamers** that there's someone in the building and they could **ambush** you!

Don't shoot

Sometimes **not** shooting at an opponent can be a clever tactic. If you spot a player in the distance who hasn't seen you, don't feel you **have** to take them out. Another gamer may do it for you and you won't reveal your location.

Tyre tip

Falling from a great height can eliminate you from the game. But falling onto a stack of black car tyres will break your fall and you'll **bounce on** to fight another battle. Jump on tyres from the ground and you also get the 'jump' on an enemy!

Crazy pyramid

Building an inverted pyramid-type base can help you take out enemies from the ground. Build two walls on all four sides, then place sloping inverted roof pieces all the way round. Now you can see 360 degrees around and **snipe the oppo**!

Bush battle

Discover the **legendary bush consumable** and Victory Royale could be in sight! Disguising yourself as a bush makes it very difficult for others to see you and you could make some easy combat kills. Don't run around though - a moving bush is a **rubbish tactic**!

FORTNITE FACT!

If you take any kind of damage while hiding as a bush, your disguise will **disappear**.

Act on impulse

Impulse grenade is a weapon that can be **lobbed at players** and its explosion will fling them into the air. The enemy may take fall damage if they are at height. It's a **clever combat tip** to get people camping (hiding) in buildings out in the open towards the end of a battle.

CLOSE-UP COMBAT

Close quarters fighting can happen at any time from the moment you land. Be prepared with this expert guide!

In close-up gunfights in the open, you don't really want to aim down the sights of your weapon. This makes you less mobile and **you become an easier target**.

If you're taking cover behind a wall or object with your opponent near, poke out and **aim for a quick headshot** before ducking back for cover.

Fortnite is a third-person perspective fighting game. This means you can see your hero and the whole scene around them. **Use this to your advantage** and work out where's safe to go.

If you land right next to other players and can't get a weapon, remember you can eliminate using just your pickaxe. It takes **several swipes** but you'll get the job done.

If you need to defend yourself and grab precious seconds to work out your next move, **jump and move around**. As a moving target you're much harder to hit.

With a weapon like a suppressed machine gun, you don't need to be super accurate close up. Spray away and **shoot from the hip** the moment an opponent appears in front of you.

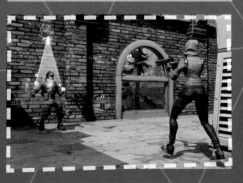

Faced with an opponent who jumps and then shoots, **quickly place a wall down** as they jump up and hopefully you'll defend the shot.

Never run away into a building if you come under gunfire from an enemy right in front of you. You could be **trapped and easily taken out**!

Roll out a boogie bomb, which is a rare ranged weapon, and it'll make your opponent **dance for five seconds**.

TRAP TRICKS AND TIPS

Damage traps are one of the most epic items in Battle Royale! They are not common, so they can be tricky to master and utilize to the max.

A damage trap is a spiked tile that can be laid on the floor, wall or ceiling of a building. If the enemy moves over or in front of it, the trap will explode and cause game-changing damage. Fortunately you can't accidentally set it off and hurt yourself!

FORTNITE FACT!

Other players can **destroy** damage traps using weapons.

The trick is to **set some exciting loot** next to a damage trap in a building and hope that an eager opponent rushes in for it. You could also set the trap and make someone chase you right over it. This is a risky technique as you're likely to come under fire.

Here is a **simple trap tip** that can catch out inexperienced gamers. Just drop a weapon or item that you don't need, retreat and hide and when another player comes along to pick it up you can take a shot at them. Simple!

C4 remote explosives can help you set a brilliant trap! It's a **rare ranged weapon** that can be found in places like supply llamas, drops and chests. C4 needs to be attached to a structure and is blown up remotely, potentially taking out enemies and buildings.

If you're a quick builder, it is possible to **build around an enemy** and trap them in! Get above them and put floors across the enemy's stairs. The perfect finishing touch is sticking a damage trap down for your opponent to set off without knowing. Boom!

! FORTNITE FACT!

Traps don't take up **any space** in your inventory.

SPECIALS AND SECRETS

Game makers Epic are always adding special new things and updates to Battle Royale. Here are just some of the best!

The awesome **thermal scope assault rifle** was released in 2018. It detects enemy heat, chests and supply drops and in legendary status creates 37 base damage. Hiding from this weapon is very difficult!

Epic boosted Battle Royale's **replay** mode and you can now use drone cameras, super slow-mo, quick-time functions and heaps more gadgets. Capturing your best in-game moments is super slick! Just go to the Career tab and select replays to check it out.

If you spot a **vending machine** around the island, take a look at the cool items you could collect! They'll cost you between 100 to 500 of wood, metal or brick materials. Give it a bash with your pickaxe and see what's on offer.

With enough skill (and practice!) you can **ride a guided missile** and fly through the sky. Shoot the missile and then guide it back at yourself at a low and flat pathway. Then you must detach and try to jump onboard. Have a nice trip!

Discover a **cozy campfire** and you can heal yourself, plus any team-mates in duos or squads. It's a rare trap item and will heal 2HP per second, lasting for 25 seconds.

Fire hydrants can be smashed open and shooting water jets can blast you up - even onto buildings. Next time you spot one, give it a go!

! FORTNITE FACT!

Legendary jetpacks let you zoom through the air. They made their first limited time appearance in 2018 - let's hope they return!

In **2018,** Epic invited Fortnite fans to show off their cool dance routines and share with them on social media. They gave prizes to the best 100, with the number one move being made into an emote in the game!

TEAM UP!

Battle Royale isn't all about solo play - team up in duos or squads and aim for Victory Royale with your friends!

In the pre-game lobby, select duos or squads and invite players you know from your friends list. You can also use auto fill to either pair you up with an unknown player, or three others in squad mode.

! **FORTNITE FACT!**

You can see the **health** and **armour** status of your team-mates.

In the game you'll know who your team-mates are because their names will appear **above their heads**. Learn to focus on attacking and taking out the enemy - don't get spooked out by your **own** team!

In team games, duos always play against other duos and squads take on other squads. You don't have to have a full squad of four, but playing with just three heroes puts you at a **massive disadvantage**!

Epic loves to release **Limited Time Modes** (LTM) which are games that can be played for just a short time, typically a week or so. **Teams of 20** sees five 20-player squads battle for glory and there has even been a manic 50 vs 50 version!

Working as a team, a **top tactic** is for two of you to rush the enemy and attack while the other two take cover and play as snipers. You'll hit the enemy **hard** and cause **total mayhem**! Use a cozy campfire to restore any health damage.

If you take down someone in duos or squads, don't **always** rush to finish them off or loot their goodies. Other enemy members may rush to the scene and you can fire shots at them as well. Great team-work, guys!

Solo Showdowns are special LTM games. In the first blitz showdown event of 2018, the battle was much quicker than normal. The storm circle was rapid and the top players earned V-Bucks depending on their kills and placement over 25 ultra-exciting matches!

Top 3 team tips «««« ««««

1 Land together.

2 Communicate all the time.

3 Share healing items.

IN-GAME EXTRAS

There are all kinds of ways of maximizing your Fortnite fun, but some will cost you money IRL...

V-Bucks is the in-game cash used in Fortnite. You have to use real money to buy V-Bucks in the game's shop. V-Bucks let you upgrade things like your character's skins, tools, gliders, emotes and other cosmetics that help your character stand out in combat on the island.

FORTNITE FACT!

Remember you don't **need** passes, V-Bucks or to complete challenges to enjoy a fun game of Fortnite Battle Royale!

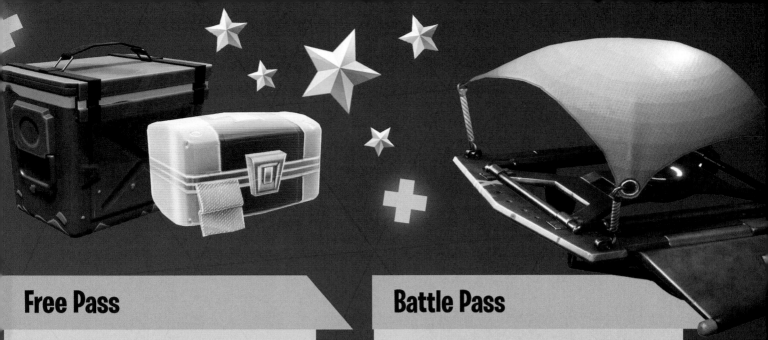

Free Pass

Players can take advantage of the **free pass** rewards system in Battle Royale. Complete set challenges to unlock a low level of free things, including icons, emotes and a small amount of V-Bucks. The free pass is free (obvs!) and the challenges can be quite basic. The more you do, the higher tier level you'll reach.

Battle Pass

The **battle pass** is an extended version of the free pass and must be bought with V-Bucks. The battle pass rewards on offer can include screens, gliders, tools and sprays as well as icons, skins and emotes.

Battle Stars

Players win **battle stars** based on the weekly challenges or daily quests they carry out. To make it to a higher tier, you must win a set amount of battle stars. Take a look in the lobby to see all the challenges that are listed.

Seasons

Battle passes are based around a **season** in Fortnite. A season will usually last two or three months and to take part in each season you must buy the new battle pass with V-Bucks. You can join a season at any point, but it makes more sense to join around the time it begins.

Finally, in each **season** you play you can boost your experience (XP). This will make your season level rise. Season XP is mainly controlled by how well you do in matches, how long you survive and how many eliminations you make.

PLANET ATTACK!

The world's threatened by strange monsters,
and only you and your team can protect it!
Get to know the basics of Fortnite Save the World...

TOP TIPS

! This PvE is for solo players or teams of up to four. You must **complete missions** and fight zombie monsters known as husks.

! The missions will see you make **epic builds** and defend locations or attempt to rescue survivors among the monsters!

! Your storm shield is a **permanent base** that you build. Items can be stored in the storm shield.

! There are **four types of heroes** to play as - soldier, constructor, outlander and ninja.

! You **harvest** metal, stone and wood materials as well as other items like twine, nuts and bolts and ores.

! Crafting is a **big part** of Save the World but you must find schematics (plans) of the things you want to craft.

! Heroes can **level up** by completing quests and earning XP.

KNOW THE ENEMY

It's time to meet the main monsters you'll come under attack from in Save the World... prepare to face your fears!

Husks

The **most common enemies** in this Fortnite PvE game look like they're wearing hoodies, but they actually have stretched skin and faces. Urgh!

FORTNITE FACT!

Standard husks use **melee attacks**, which means they use their hands to inflict damage.

Husky

Wider and stronger than the usual husk, a husky can **damage buildings** as well as players.

Chrome Husky

These metallic-looking husks have a higher defence power and can **revive after death** unless they are taken out by fire or water.

Pitcher

Watch out for pitcher husks! These baseball-loving dudes will **throw bones at you** and if they team up can cause a lot of hurt.

Mimic Monster

Mimic monsters are crazy creatures that look like chests. After being searched, they **transform** and will attack heroes!

FORTNITE FACT!

Blasters have **laser eyes** that can zap you from a long distance.

Mist Monsters

Mist monsters are less common than husks, but are bigger and unleash more damage! **Smashers, takers, blasters** and **flingers** are four types of terrifying mist monsters. Flingers have one larger arm and will chuck husks using their mega power!

Rescue the Survivors
STRATEGY AND TIPS!

Saving survivors is one of the coolest and most fun missions.
Here are some top tips to help your quest!

FORTNITE FACT!

Rescue the Survivors mission is a **great** way to increase the power of your home base.

The aim is to rescue six survivors in a set time of 20 minutes. The clock's **always ticking** and you'll need a good stack of weapons to complete the task. The assault rifle is the best all-round gun in survivor searching.

If you're close enough to a survivor they will often appear on your mini map as a **blue shape**. So keep checking your map as it can be an easy way to pick up the people you're after!

Search **high and low**! Survivors can be hiding at the top of tall buildings in city locations, or lurking in basements and underground positions. You need to be an **epic explorer** in this mission!

Survivors may be found behind big shelves or supply areas or they may hide in the corners of rooms. Keep your eyes peeled and **peek everywhere** for the six dudes you're trying to save!

Always have a melee weapon at your disposal, like a sword or spear, to help you in **close-up combat**. If you run out of ammo, your guns will be no use against husks!

Other **exciting** regular Save the World missions include storm shield defending, destroying encampments and escort and evacuation missions.

Survivors can be heard calling and shouting out to you in the game. **Use a headset** and their voices can help you home in on their location.

CRAFTING AND BUILDING

These are two very important parts to Save the World, so check out these sneaky tips.

In Save the World, your weapons have a **durability level**. This is shown on the top right of the screen. You'll need to craft and replace a weapon using schematics when it **wears down**.

Scavenge for nuts and bolts, which are **essential building materials**, from parking meters on the roadside. These are super easy to smash and always harvest a few nuts and bolts. Cars, tool boxes and rusted cans are also good sources.

!

FORTNITE FACT!

Loot large tool boxes first before you **smash** them up for materials!

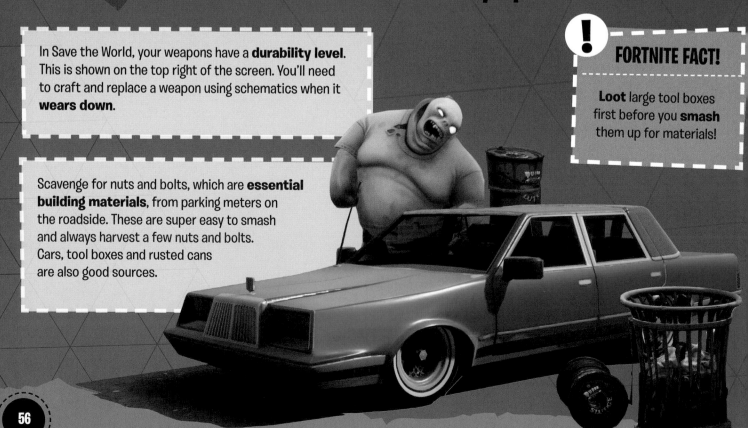

If you build walls around an objective, remember that husks will **target** the weakest walls that you haven't upgraded. Try to upgrade all walls if you can.

If you've harvested enough wood, create a tall ramp and lay floor tiles to help you cover **large distances** over tall objects like buildings and forests. Just don't fall off as you'll suffer fall damage!

Buildings with basements can be **very** handy structures! Destroy the building, including the floor, leaving just the basement. It will be a great place to trap husks - just remember to **take out any stairs** in the basement.

Structures called **kill tunnels** can really damage enemy monsters! They are basic boxes that have two wall tiles, a floor and floor tile as a roof. Set a trap inside this small tunnel and watch the **carnage** when husks enter!

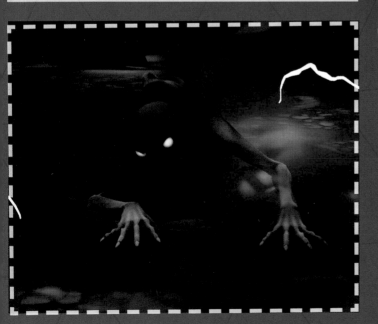

WEAPONS AT THE READY!

As always in Fortnite, knowing how to boss weapons is crucial!

Your basic **pickaxe** is a tool for harvesting materials, but it's still a weapon! Husks usually don't like it when you wave an axe in front of them!

Swords are perfect for speedy attacks in close-up combat. Their damage can be low, but their strike rate's high and they'll scare (and smash) husks to pieces! Use a heavy sword when faced with crowds of monsters.

Hardware melee weapons include sledges and crowbars. But pull out a heavy hammer if your aim is to quickly bash up a small group of monsters!

Assault rifles are suitable for all hero classes, but soldiers are definitely the top match to this versatile weapon. Use the schematic for a burst assault rifle and target husks precisely with accurate, short-round firing.

With a mag size of 30, **auto pistols** can be an effective weapon when zapping zombies in close quarters and some mid-range battles. With a quick reload speed and high DPS, pistols are **more useful** here than in Battle Royale.

Heavy shotguns look awesome in face-to-face missions with monsters. Go for the copper room sweeper heavy shotgun and you'll really make the most of its 20 mag size, 63 damage and 90 impact.

Explosive weapons fall into two categories - **grenade launchers** and **rocket launchers**. Use grenades to stun groups of husks that are quite close to your base. Rockets are fired from long distances and deal greater damage and impact. They are single shot though, so choose when to fire **very** carefully!

SAVE THE WORLD

Epic Save the World tips!

Don't always **upgrade the schematics** on weapons too far. They will cost more crafting materials to replace.

If you're a ninja, do a **double jump** move just before landing from a big height and your fall damage will be much less.

Destroy the walls on first floor buildings first and the rest of the structure should crumble easily. A simple technique but very effective!

Players can **select two gadgets** before a mission. The supply drop gadget is ultra useful for instantly collecting materials without needing to leave your base.

You can get hold of **llama piñatas** through levelling up in the game, or purchasing with V-Bucks. Give them a whack and collect the items they drop – these crazy dudes are full of sweet survival supplies!

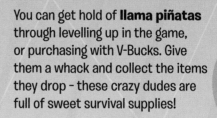

Placing duplicate and unwanted items in the **collection book** will boost your XP. But remember, you can't take stuff back once it's placed in the book.

Don't forget to **craft ammo** while you're shooting it out in a gunfight. Console players need to hold down the reload button to do this.

Have a clear **line of sight** around your base. Clear things such as nearby walls, buildings and trees so that you can defend your objective much more easily.

MY FORTNITE
RECORDS, FAVES AND FACTS

Fill in your best bits, stats and facts as you battle through Fortnite!

My name:

....

My age:

....

Year I started playing Fortnite:

....

I play...

Battle Royale ☐   Save the World ☐   Both ☐

I love Fortnite because...

....

....

Fave Battle Royale location:

....

My fave skin:

....

My fave weapon:

....

Most kills in a battle:

....

I have .... Victory Royales

EPIC EMOTES!

Dance emotes are an awesome part of Fortnite.
Tick these off if your hero character pulls them out!

Floss ☐

Dab ☐

Chicken ☐

Disco Fever ☐

Electro Shuffle ☐

Gun Show ☐

Thumbs Up ☐

Slow Cap ☐

Rock Paper Scissors ☐

Brush Your Shoulders ☐

Snap ☐

Fresh ☐